How To Tell The Birds From The Flowers
And Other Wood-cuts.

A Revised Manual of Flornithology for Beginners.

Verses and Illustrations
By Robert Williams Wood.

Start Publishing PD LLC
Copyright © 2024 by Start Publishing PD LLC

All rights reserved, including the right to reproduce this book or portions thereof in any form whatsoever.

Start Publishing PD is a registered trademark of Start Publishing PD LLC
Manufactured in the United States of America

Cover art: Shutterstock/Taisiya Kozorez

Cover design: Jennifer Do

10 9 8 7 6 5 4 3 2 1

ISBN 979-8-8809-0566-9

For some are guided by tradition,
While others use their intuition,
And even I make no pretense
Of having more than common sense.
Indeed these strange homologies
Are in most flornithologies,
And I have freely drawn upon
The works of Gray and Audubon,
Avoiding though the frequent blunders
Of those who study Nature's wonders.

Intro-duc-tion.

By other Nature books I'm sure,
  You've often been misled,
You've tried a wall-flower to secure,
  And "picked a hen" instead:
You've wondered what the egg-plants lay,
  And why the chestnut's burred,
And if the hop-vine hops away,
  It's perfectly absurd.
I hence submit for your inspection,
  This very new and choice collection,
Of flowers on Storks, and Phlox of birds,
  With some explanatory words.
Not every one is always able
  To recognize a vegetable,

Burr. Bird.

Who is there who has never heard,
About the Burdock and the Bird?
And yet how very very few,
Discriminate between the two,
While even Mr. Burbank can't.
Transform a Bird into a Plant.

Burbank.

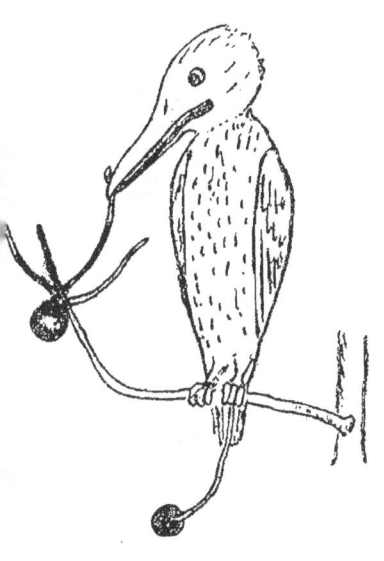 

The Crow.   The Crocus.

Some are unable, as you know,
To tell the Crocus from the Crow;
The reason why is just be-caws
They are not versed in Nature's laws.
The noisy cawing Crows all come,
Obedient to the Cro'custom,
A large Crow Caw-cus to convoke.
You never hear the Crocus croak!

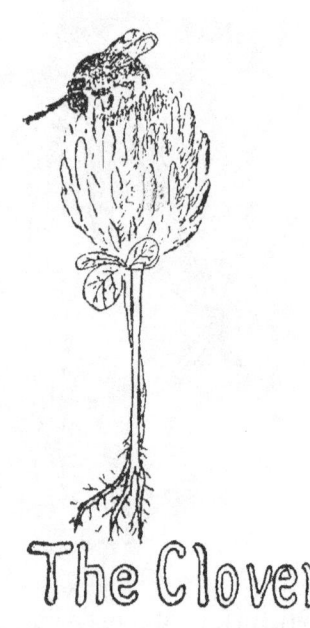

The Clover.   The Plover.

The Plover and the Clover can be told apart with ease,
By paying close attention to the habits of the Bees,
For En-to-mo-lo-gists aver, the Bee can be in Clover,
While Ety-mo-lo-gists concur, there is no B in Plover.

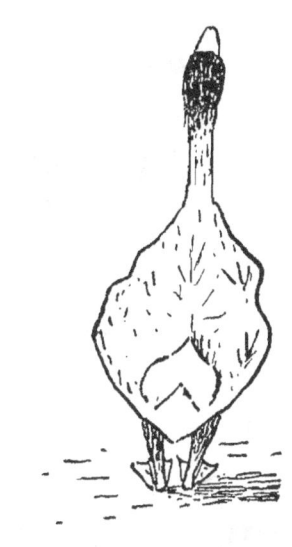 

The Ole Gander. The Oleander.

The Gander loves to promenade.
Around the farmer's poultry yard,
While as we see, the Oleander
Is quite unable to meander:
The Gardener tied it up indeed.
Fearing that it might run to seed.

 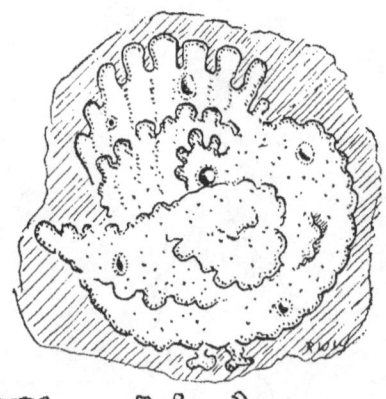

The Hen.   The Lichen.

Lichens, regardless of conventions,
Exist in only two dimensions,
A life restricted to a plane,
On rocks and stones a greenish stain,
They live upon the simplest fare,
A drop of dew, a breath of air.
Contrast them with the greedy Hen,
And her most careless regimen,
She shuns the barren stones and rocks,
And thrives upon the garbage box.

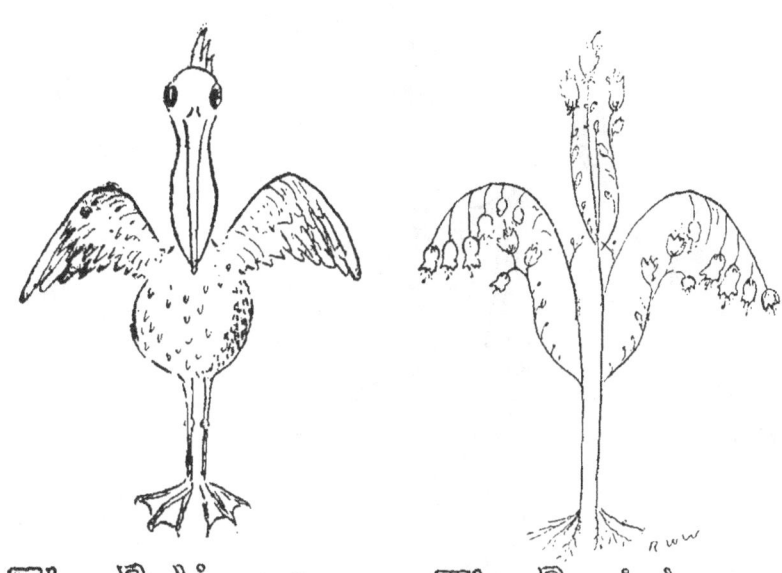

The Pelican.   The Panicle.

The Panicle and Pelican have
  often been confused,
The letters which spell Pelican,
  in Panicle are used.
If you recognize this Anagram you'll
  never go astray,
Or make the careless blunder that
  was made by Mr. Gray.

The Pea.   The Pewee.

To tell the Pewee from the Pea,
Requires great per-spi-ca-city.
Here in the pod we see the Pea,
While perched close by is the Pewee;
The Pea he hears the Pewee peep,
While Pewee sees the wee Pea weep,
There'll be but little time to see,
How Pewee differs from the Pea.

The Parrot.   The Carrot.

The Parrot and the Carrot one may
                easily confound,
They're very much alike in looks
                and similar in sound,
We recognize the Parrot by his
                clear articulation,
For Carrots are unable to engage
                in conversation.

The Rue.   The Rooster.

When you awake at half-past-two,
And hear a "Cock-a-doodle-doo,"
No argument need then ensue,
It is the Rooster, not the Rue,
Which never thus disturbs our dreams
With ruthless rude nocturnal screams
We sleep less soundly than we used ter
And love the Rue but rue the Rooster.

The Hawk. The Hollyhock.

To recognize this bird-of-prey,
The broody hen you should survey:
She takes her chicks on daily walks,
Among the neighboring Hollyhocks,
While with the Hawk association,
Is quite beyond her toleration.

The Pecan. The Toucan.

Very few can
Tell the Toucan
From the Pecan —
Here's a new plan:
To take the Toucan from the tree,
Requires immense a-gil-i-tee,
While anyone can pick with ease
The Pecans from the Pecan trees.
It's such an easy thing to do,
That even the Toucan he can too.

 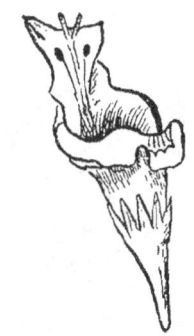

The Cat-bird.   The Cat-nip.

The Cat-bird's call resembles that
Emitted by the Pussy Cat,
While Cat-nip growing by the wall,
Is never known to caterwaul:
It's odor though attracts the Kits,
And throws them in Cat-nip-tion fits.

The Quail.   The Kale.

The California Quail is said.
To have a tail upon his head,
While contrary-wise we style the Kale,
A cabbage-head upon a tail.
It is not hard to tell the two,
The Quail commences with a queue.

The Auk. The Orchid.

We seldom meet, when out to walk,
Either the Orchid or the Auk.
The awk-ward Auk is only known
To dwellers in the Auk-tic zone,
While Orchids can be found in legions,
Within the equatorial regions.
So if by chance you travel on
The Lena or the Amazon,
Be certain of the tem-pera-ture
Or you will make mistakes I'm sure.

The Cow Bird.   The Cowslip.

Although the Cow's lips on this plant,
Suggest perhaps a ru-min-ant,
One never sees the opening bud,
Devour the grass or chew its cud.
The Cowbird picture, I suspect,
Is absolutely incorrect;
We make such errors now and then,
A sort of cow slip of the pen.

The Butter-ball.   The Butter-cup.

The little Butter-cup can sing,
From morn 'till night like anything.
The quacking of the Butter-ball,
Cannot be called a song at all.
We thus the flower may learn to know,
Its song is reproduced below.

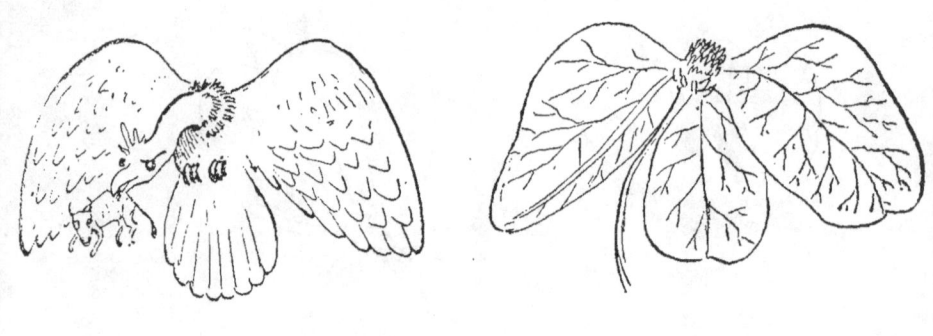

The Roc.   The Shamrock

Although I never took much stock,
In Sinbad's yarn about the Roc,
And really must confess I am
Inclined to think the Roc a sham:
Take notice that, the Sham-rock may
Be seen upon St Patrick's day.

 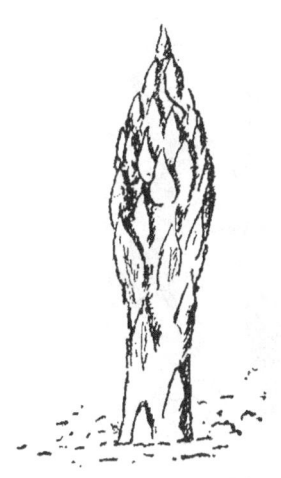

A Sparrer.   Asparagus.

Of the fall of the Sparrow we often have heard,
And I've here represented the fall of the bird:
In the case of Asparagus though, I may mention,
A fall such as this, is quite out of the question:
For observe that Asparagus, fat and well fed,
Spends all of his time in the 'sparagus bed.

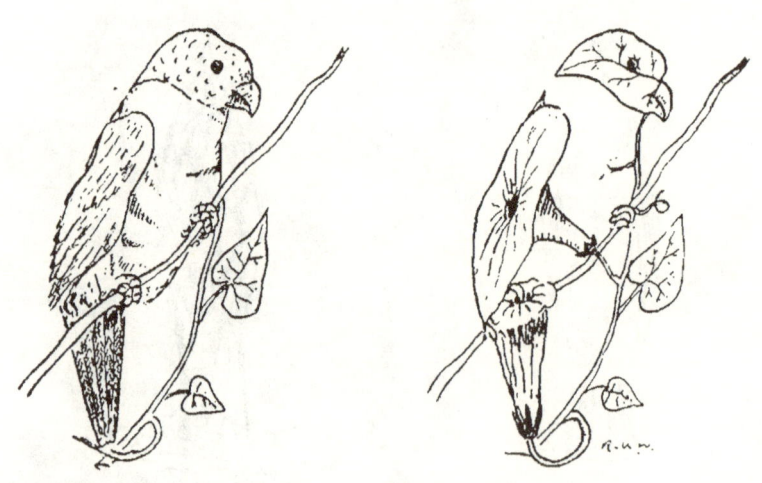

The Blue Mountain Lory. The Blue Morning Glory.

The Insects, to avoid surprise
By Birds, sometimes themselves disguise
As leaves and twigs, and thus escape
The appetizing Insect's fate.
Observe how cleverly this Vine
Has forced its leaves and flowers to twine
Themselves into a Bird design.
And how it's artful turns and twists,
Hides it from zealous Botanists.

While as we see, the Tern is not:
He is not always doomed to be
Thus bound to earth e-<u>tern</u>-ally
For "cooked to a tern" may be inferred.
To change the Turnip to a bird.

Observe the Turnip in the Pot.
The Tern is glad that he is not!

 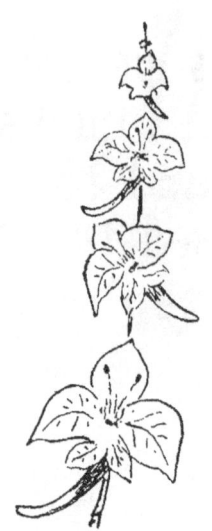

The Larks.   The Larkspur.

You must not make ad-verse remarks,
About my drawing of the Larks.
For, by the minor poet's lore
The Larks-per-pet-ually soar.
While Larkspurs, bordering garden walks,
Are perched securely on their stalks.

Cross Bill.   Sweet William.

Nobody but an imbecile
Mistakes Sweet William for Cross Bill:
And even I can scarcely claim,
The skill to make them look the same.
Some other shrubs and vines and trees,
Express emotion much like these,
You've seen the mad-wort plant I guess,
And weeping willows and sigh-press,
The passion-flower, at it's climax,
The glad-iolus and the smile-ax.

The Ibis.   The Ibiscus.

The sacred Ibis, one might say,
Was classified a "Bird-of-Pray"
His body, after death, was dried,
Embalmed in pitch, and mummyfied,
And thus was handed down to us
In some old King's sarcophagus.
The Mallow, growing in the bogs,
('Ibiscus termed by pedagogues)
Is much opposed to dessication,
And bears no marks of veneration.

The Pipe.   The Snipe.

Observe the hybrid Indian Pipe,
Likewise the high-bred English Snipe,
Who is distinguished, as we see,
By his superior pedigree.

Two crosses botonny
Bend sinister

Fess Argent
Martlets Sable.

The Jay.   The Bay.

The Blue Jay, as we clearly see,
Is so much like the green Bay tree
That one might say the only clue
Lies in their dif-fer-ence of hue,
And if you have a color sense,
You'll see at once this difference.

The Gent-ians. The Lady-bird.

The reason why this beetle gay,
Is called the Lady-bird, they say,
Is just because he wastes his hours,
In running after pretty flowers,
Who, quite regardless of conventions,
Most openly invite attentions.
(And hence are aptly termed the Gent-ians)

Puffin.   Nuffin.

Upon this cake of ice is perched,
   The paddle-footed puffin:
To find his double I have searched,
   But have discovered — Nuffin'.

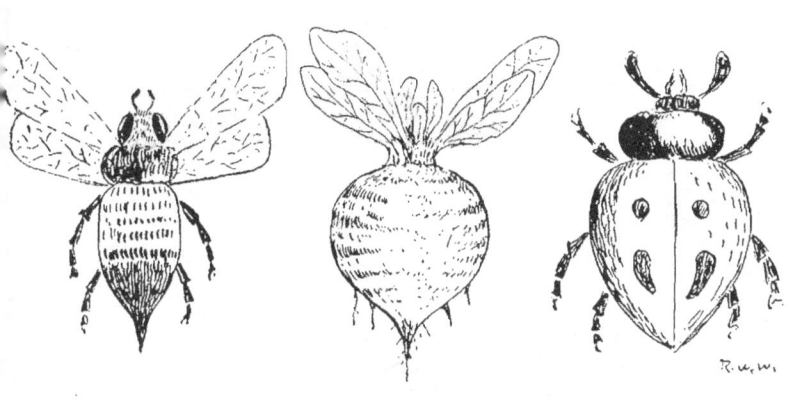

The Bee. The Beet. The Beetle.

Good Mr. Darwin once contended
That Beetles were from Bees descended,
And as my pictures show I think
The Beet must be the missing link.
The sugar-beet and honey-bee
Supply the Beetle's pedigree:
The family is now complete,—
The Bee, the Beetle and the Beet.

 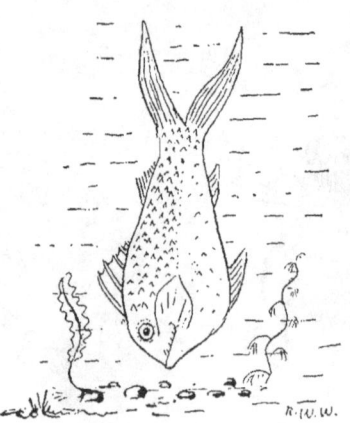

The Bunny. The Tunny.

The superficial naturalists have
    often been misled,
By failing to discriminate between
    the tail and head:
It really is unfortunate such
    carelessness prevails,
Because the Bunnies have their
heads where Tunnies have their tails.

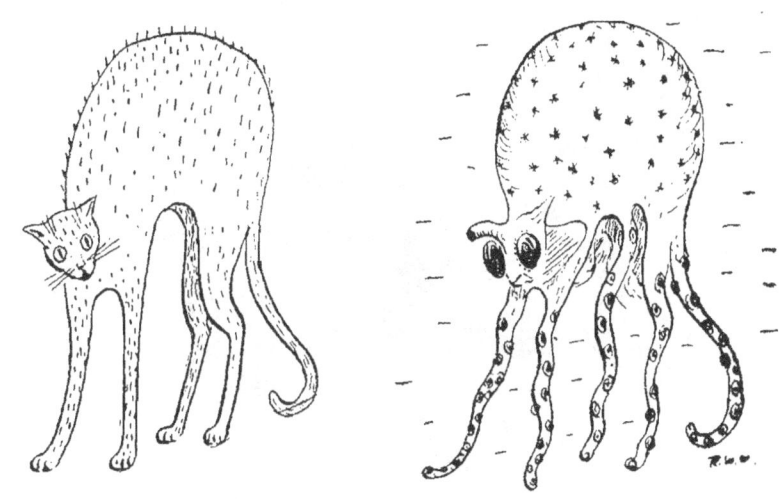

The Puss.   The Octo-pus.

The Octopus or Cuttle-fish!
I'm sure that none of us would wish
To have him scuttle 'round the house,
Like Puss, when she espies a mouse:
When <u>you</u> secure your house-hold pet,
Be very sure you do not get
The Octopus, or there may be
Domestic in-<u>felis</u>-ity.

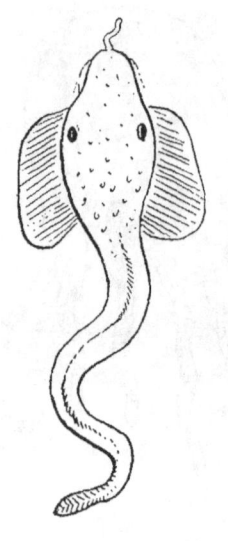 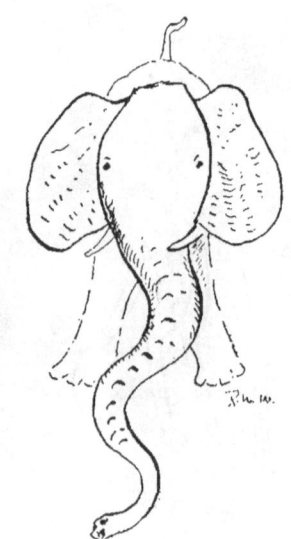

The Eel.   The Eelephant.

The marked aversion which we feel,
When in the presence of the Eel,
Makes many view with consternation
The Elephant's front ele-vation.
Such folly must be clearly due
To their peculiar point of view.

The Ant. The Pheas-ant.

The ant is known by his ant-ennae,
Where-as the pheas-ant hasn't any,
And that is why he wears instead,
A small red cap upon his head:
Without his Fez, indeed the pheasant,
Would be quite bald and quite un-pleasant.

The Hare.   The Harrier.

The Harrier, harassed by the Hare,
Presents a picture of despair;
Although as far as I'm concerned,
I love to see the tables turned.
The Harrier flies with all his might,
It is a harum-scare'm flight:
I'm not surprised he does not care
To meet the fierce pursuing Hare.

 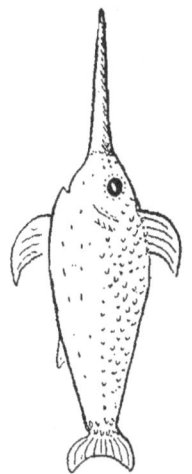

The Pen-guin. The Sword-fish.

We have for many years been bored
By that old saw about the sword
And pen, and now we all rejoice,
To see how Nature made her choice:
She made, regardless of offendin',
The Sword-fish mightier than the Penguin.

The Gnu.   The Newt.

The Gnu conspicuously wears.
His coat of gnumerous bristling hairs,
While, as we see, the modest Newt
Of such a coat is destitute.
(I'm only telling this to you,
And it is strictly "entre gnu")
In point of fact the Newt is nude,
And therefore he does not obtrude,
But hides in some secluded gnook,
Beneath the surface of the brook.

It's almost more than he can bear,
To issue slyly from his lair,
And snatch a hasty breath of air,
His need of which is absolute,
Because, you see, he is a pneu-t.*

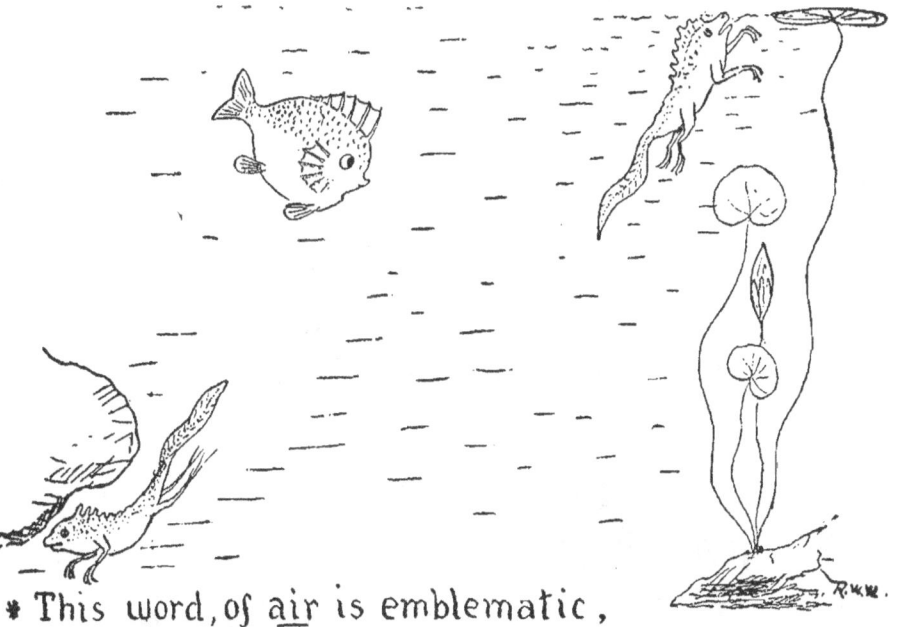

* This word, of <u>air</u> is emblematic,
  Greek, "pneumos"- air- compare Pneumatic.

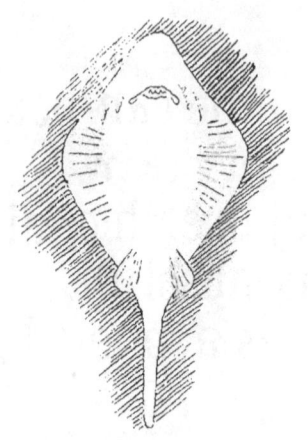 

I always sing the hymn of hate,
When I perceive the Ray (or skate)
His ugly mouth I can't abide,
His eyes are on the other side,
His features are all out of place
He hasn't even any face.
I do not mind the Raven, though
Maligned by Edgar Allan Poe:

By his fun-er-ial array
We recognize him from the Ray,
Whose epiderm is white as snow,
Not black as night, like Mr Crow.
Though black, morose, and quite
  unshaven
I'm sure we all prefer the Raven.

The Ape   The Grape.

The Apes, from whom we are descended,
Hang ape-x down from trees suspended,
And since we find them in the trees,
We term them arbor-ig-i-nes.
This quite explains the monkey-shines
Cut up by those who pluck from vines
The Grape, and then subject its juices,
To Bacchanalian abuses.

The Doe.   The Dodo.

The Doe and her phonetic double,
No longer are a source of trouble,
Because the Dodo, it appears,
Has been extinct for many years:
She was too haughty to embark,
With total strangers in Noah's ark,
And we rejoice because her pride,
Our nature book has simplified.

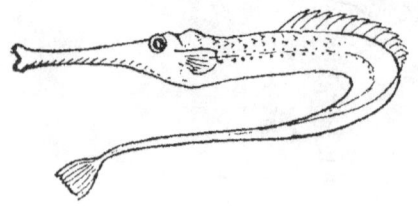 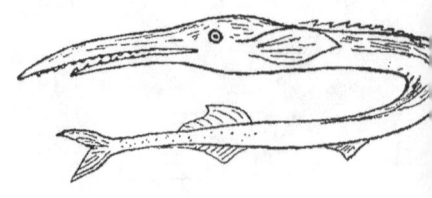

The Pipe-fish.   The Sea-gar.

To smoke a herring is to make
  A most lam-en-table mistake,
Particularly since there are
  The Pipe-fish and the long Sea-gar.
Bear this in mind when next you wish
  To smoke your after-dinner fish.

The Elk.   The Whelk.

A roar of welkome through the welkin.
Is certain proof you'll find the Elk in;
But if you listen to the shell,
In which the Whelk is said to dwell,
And hear a roar, beyond a doubt
It indicates the Whelk is out.

The P-Cock. The Q-Cumber.

The striking similarity of this
          P-Q-liar pair,
No longer need en-cumber us,
       or fill us with despair:
The P-Cock and the Q-Cumber
      you never need confuse,
If you pay attention to the Eyes
      and mind your P's and Q's.

The Sloe.   The Sloth.

See what a fix the Sloth is in,
He has been captured by the gin:
This gin is not the same gin though,
In which we sometimes find the Sloe.
This shows how careful one must be,
To treat the gin most gingerly.

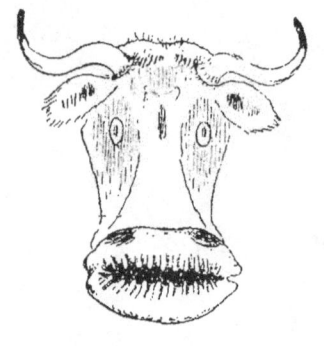 

The Cow.   The Cowry.

The Cowry seems to be, somehow,
A sort of mouth-piece for the Cow:
A speaking likeness one might say,
Which I've endeavored to portray.

The Antelope. The Cantelope.

If you will tap the Cantelope
    reposing on the ground
It will not move, but just emit
    a melon-choly sound
But if you try this method on
    the antlered antelope,
His departure will convince you
    that he is a misanthrope.

The Pansy.   The Chim-pansy.

Observe how Nature's necromancies
Have clearly painted on the Pansies,
These almost human counten-ances,
In yellow, blue and black nu-ances.
The face however seems to me
To be that of the Chim-pan-zee:
A fact that makes the gentle Pansy,
Appeal no longer to my fancy.

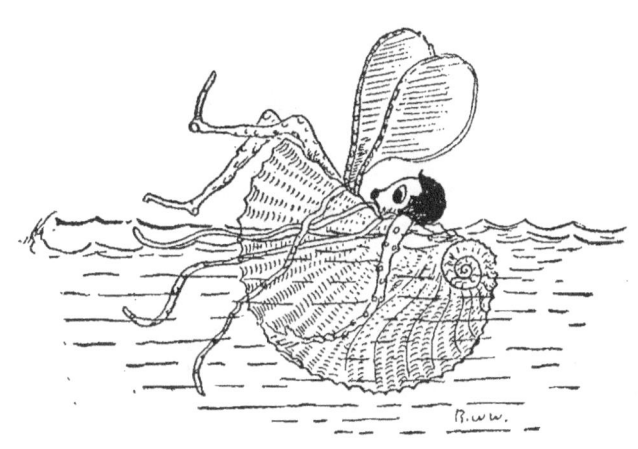

Naught. Nautilus.

The Argo-naut or Nautilus,
With habits quite adventurous,
A com-bin-a-tion of a snail,
A jelly-fish and paper sail.
The parts of him that did not jell,
Are packed securely in his shell.
It is not strange that when I sought
To find his double, I found Naught.

www.ingramcontent.com/pod-product-compliance
Lightning Source LLC
Chambersburg PA
CBHW031434040426
42444CB00006B/802